1 9 8 8
The Year You Were Born

Birth Certificate

Name: Rachel Korn

Birthdate: 8/16/88

Time: 10:15

Place of Birth: _____

Weight: _____ Length: _____

Mother's maiden name: Miller

Father's name: Korn

For Caroline Martinet, from her Auntie Jeanne J.M.

To Mark Paski and Muffin J.L.

Text copyright ©1995 by Jeanne Martinet
Illustrations copyright © 1995 by Judy Lanfredi

Inquiries should be addressed to Tambourine Books,
a division of William Morrow & Company, Inc.,
1350 Avenue of the Americas, New York, New York 10019.
Printed in the United States of America.

ISBN 0-688-13862-4 (pbk.)   ISBN 0-688-13861-6 (lib. bdg.)

1   3   5   7   9   10   8   6   4   2
First edition

1 9 8 8
The Year You Were Born

Compiled by

JEANNE MARTINET

Illustrated by

JUDY LANFREDI

Tambourine Books · New York

U.S. Almanac
1988

World population 5,112,000,000

United States population 246,329,000
Males 120,203,000
Females 126,126,000

Households 91,066,000

Size of the U.S. 3,618,770 square miles

President Ronald Reagan

Biggest state (in area)
Alaska, 591,004 square miles

State with most cows Texas, with 13,500,000

State with most pigs Iowa, with 13,800,000

Longest river
Mississippi-Missouri, 3,710 miles

Number of births in the U.S.
Boys 2,002,000
Girls 1,907,000
Average weight at birth 7 pounds, 7 ounces

Deaths in the U.S. 2,168,000

Tornadoes 702

Households with TV sets
89,000,000
Number of TV stations 1,030

Households with VCRs 51,000,000

Average number of hours each week kids
ages 2 to 11 watch TV
31 hours, 52 minutes

Fax machines sold 1,000,000

Top nonalcoholic beverage
Milk, 25.8 gallons per person

Favorite U.S. snack Potato chips

Boy Scouts 4,228,000

Girl Scouts 2,345,000

Most popular girl's name
Ashley

Most popular boy's name
Michael

Most popular sport played
Swimming: 66,000,000 people in the U.S.
over 7 years old are swimmers.

Top pet Cats, 57,500,000

Children's books sold 244,000,000

Number of different magazines published
11,566

Cars and trucks made in 1988
13,000,000

Total length of railroad tracks in the U.S.
184,235 miles

January

*J*anuary is named after Janus, the Roman god of doorways and of beginnings.

BIRTHSTONE *Garnet*

FRIDAY
January 1

New Year's Day • As part of a celebration of the 200th anniversary of the settlement of Australia, a train of 10 camels arrives in Adelaide, South Australia, after a 117-day trek from the north coast. • President Ronald Reagan and Soviet leader Mikhail Gorbachev exchange friendly greetings on television.

SATURDAY
January 2

An oil storage tank collapses and empties 860,000 gallons of oil into the Monongahela River near Pittsburgh, Pennsylvania, causing a 20-mile-long oil slick.

SUNDAY
January 3

2 women who were stuck in the snow for 10 days near Springfield, Arizona, have been rescued. They stayed alive inside their snowbound truck by sharing 1 bag of peanuts and 1 sweet roll, and by drinking melted snow.

MONDAY
January 4

Full Moon

Icy air from the Arctic covers much of the U.S. It's 31° below zero in West Yellowstone, Montana!

TUESDAY
January 5

A Chinese newspaper, *China Daily*, reports that drinking a tonic made with powdered ants may cure arthritis.

WEDNESDAY
January 6

In Mechanicsburg, Pennsylvania, 10-year-old Girl Scout Jessica Muce wins a Girl Scout Cookie–eating contest. She eats 5 Thin Mints in 1 minute.

THURSDAY
January 7

A commuter plane hits a sleeping moose at the Soldotna Airport in Anchorage, Alaska.

FRIDAY
January 8

Earthquake in southern Italy. It measures 4.2 on the Richter scale. • A huge snowstorm blankets most of the U.S.

SATURDAY
January 9

ZOO NEWS: A callimico, also called a Goeldi's monkey, is born at the Brookfield Zoo near Chicago, Illinois. It is the 200th callimico born there in the past 10 years.

WHO ELSE WAS BORN IN JANUARY?
LOUIS BRAILLE

French musician, teacher
Blind at age 3, he invented the raised-dot system
of writing that is now used by most blind people.
BORN   January 4, 1809, in Coupvray, France

SUNDAY
January 10

13,000 scouts attend the World Boy Scout Jamboree in
Australia. • Today is the anniversary of the discovery of oil in
Texas in 1901.

MONDAY
January 11

The water is turned back on in many homes in Ohio,
Pennsylvania, and West Virginia. Water service has been
disrupted because of the oil tank spill on January 2.

TUESDAY
January 12

The new prime minister of Japan, Noboru Takeshita, arrives in
Washington, D.C., for his first visit to the U.S. • In
Cincinnati, Ohio, City Council members show up at a public
hearing wearing pig snouts and pig ears!

WEDNESDAY
January 13

A 71-pound tail cone falls off a plane during landing at the Dallas–
Fort Worth International Airport in Texas. No one is hurt.

THURSDAY
January 14

In San Francisco, California, artist Gary Sussman
carves a huge statue of a gold miner from 1849 out
of a 6,000-pound block of Ivory soap.

FRIDAY
January 15

Hat Day • People in the town of Hull,
Massachusetts, are listening to the broadcast
from nearby WBZ—but not on their radios.
The sound is somehow coming in through
radiators, organs, telephones, and even the toilets!

SATURDAY
January 16

National Nothing Day • Officials in Los Angeles County in
California are baffled by a series of mysterious underground
explosions that rattle windows and break china.

SUNDAY
January 17

A huge cactus 57 feet, 11¾ inches high is discovered in the
Maricopa Mountains, 11 miles east of Gila Bend, Arizona. It's
a saguaro, the largest of all cacti.

BIRTHDAYS IN 1988

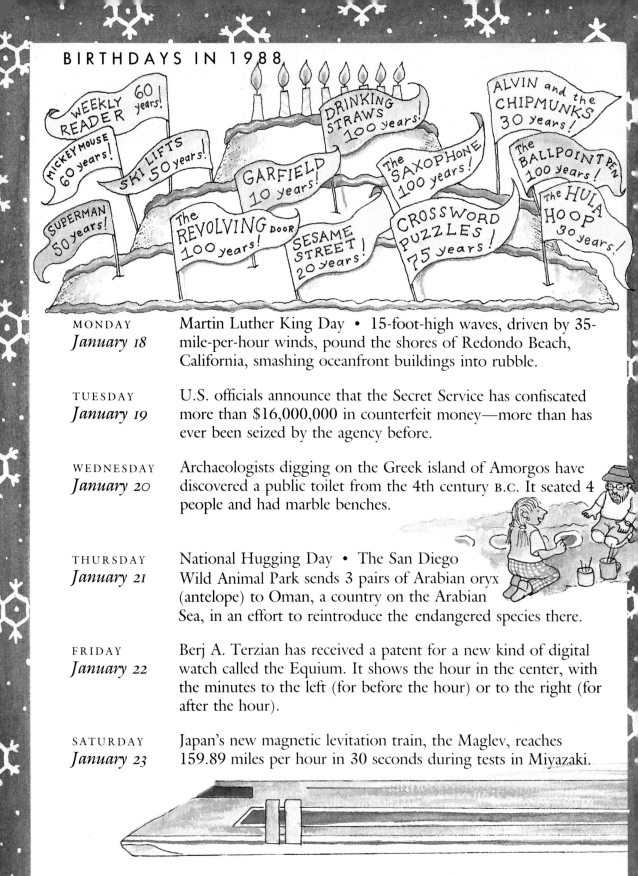

WEEKLY READER 60 years!

MICKEY MOUSE 60 years!

SKI LIFTS 50 years!

SUPERMAN 50 years!

The REVOLVING DOOR 100 years!

GARFIELD 10 years!

SESAME STREET 20 years!

DRINKING STRAWS 100 years!

The SAXOPHONE 100 years!

CROSSWORD PUZZLES 75 years!

ALVIN and the CHIPMUNKS 30 years!

The BALLPOINT PEN 100 years!

The HULA HOOP 30 years!

MONDAY
January 18

Martin Luther King Day • 15-foot-high waves, driven by 35-mile-per-hour winds, pound the shores of Redondo Beach, California, smashing oceanfront buildings into rubble.

TUESDAY
January 19

U.S. officials announce that the Secret Service has confiscated more than $16,000,000 in counterfeit money—more than has ever been seized by the agency before.

WEDNESDAY
January 20

Archaeologists digging on the Greek island of Amorgos have discovered a public toilet from the 4th century B.C. It seated 4 people and had marble benches.

THURSDAY
January 21

National Hugging Day • The San Diego Wild Animal Park sends 3 pairs of Arabian oryx (antelope) to Oman, a country on the Arabian Sea, in an effort to reintroduce the endangered species there.

FRIDAY
January 22

Berj A. Terzian has received a patent for a new kind of digital watch called the Equium. It shows the hour in the center, with the minutes to the left (for before the hour) or to the right (for after the hour).

SATURDAY
January 23

Japan's new magnetic levitation train, the Maglev, reaches 159.89 miles per hour in 30 seconds during tests in Miyazaki.

Loretta and Gerald Hoffman of Minneapolis, Minnesota, open their home to 63 people who are stranded on a highway blocked by snowdrifts. They all spend the night on the floor of the Hoffman house—and they are all given breakfast.

The oldest working magician in the U.S., Jimmy Grippo, turns 90 today. He has performed magic tricks for 70 years and once even hypnotized J. Edgar Hoover (the former head of the FBI) while President Franklin Roosevelt picked his pocket! • Mild earthquake in southern California.

HAPPY ANNIVERSARY, AUSTRALIANS!

In 1988, it is exactly 200 years since settlers from Great Britain first came to Australia. The first settlers were mostly convicts, soldiers, and government officials. To mark the anniversary, hundreds of special events are held throughout the year. The official slogan is "Let's make it great in '88!"

On January 1, 10 camels arrive in Adelaide at exactly 1 minute past midnight to start off the year's festivities. The parade of camels set out from the north coast of Australia on September 6, 1987, and have traveled straight across the heart of Australia—following the route of the first telegraph line, built in 1872. Camels were very important for exploring Australia in the 18th century because they were good at carrying people and heavy loads over vast distances.

On January 26, two million people, including the Prince and Princess of Wales, watch as fireworks fill the sky over 200 tall ships in Sydney Harbor. From April 30 to October 30, thousands visit the 98-acre World Expo in Brisbane, which features a monorail, a ski slope made with artificial snow, gem-cutting demonstrations, and many other exhibits.

The Aborigines, who had lived in Australia for thousands of years before the British arrived, demonstrate to protest the celebration.

FUN FACT '88

Antelope like to live in large herds for safety. Springbok antelope used to live in herds of over 100,000!

TUESDAY
January 26

In Indiana, 42,000 pounds of powdered carbon is dumped into the Ohio River to try to make the fuel-contaminated water safe to drink. • A nationwide study released today shows that taking aspirin may reduce the risk of heart attack.

WEDNESDAY
January 27

A giant Caesar salad is made in Tijuana, Mexico. In it are 840 heads of lettuce, 840 eggs, and 350 cups of croutons. It is tossed by Rosa Cardini, whose father invented the Caesar salad in 1924.

THURSDAY
January 28

American and Kuwaiti scientists have discovered that catfish slime, a jelly released by the fish after it is caught, has amazing healing power when used on human cuts and wounds.

FRIDAY
January 29

Hundreds of cowboys recite poetry at the annual Cowboy Poetry Gathering in Elko, Nevada. • In Buffalo, New York, the Winter-fest II snow-sculpting event is canceled due to lack of snow.

SATURDAY
January 30

In Phoenix, Arizona, America's largest park for the handicapped is dedicated; it has 2 baseball fields for the blind, and tennis and basketball courts for people in wheelchairs.

SUNDAY
January 31

The Washington Redskins beat the Denver Broncos, 42–10, in football's Super Bowl XXII.

• A Boeing 747SP sets a record for civilian round-the-world flight: 23,100 miles in 36 hours, 54 minutes, and 15 seconds. Its average speed is over 600 miles per hour.

U.S. SUPREME COURT RULES STUDENT NEWSPAPERS CAN BE CENSORED

OLDEST PERSON IN WORLD DIES AT AGE 114

INTERNATIONAL AIDS CONFERENCE IN LONDON

1,382,101 DOMINOES TOPPLED IN THE NETHERLANDS

February

*T*he name February comes from the Latin *Februa*, which means "feast of purification."

BIRTHSTONE *Amethyst*

MONDAY
February 1

A bullet factory in Laguna Hills, California, catches fire. Fire fighters are forced to stand to one side and let it burn, because bullets are flying out of the building.

TUESDAY
February 2

Full Moon

Groundhog Day • Happy 75th birthday to Grand Central Terminal in New York City. • A 2-year-old child who wandered away from his home yesterday is found in the mountains near Harrisonburg, Virginia. He is cold but okay!

WEDNESDAY
February 3

Anthony Kennedy is approved by the Senate to be a judge on the U.S. Supreme Court. • At the Cincinnati Zoo in Ohio, a rare white-breasted king-fisher chick has hatched; it's the first bird of this kind to be hatched in captivity.

THURSDAY
February 4

No Talk Day, sponsored by Garner Elementary School in Clio, Michigan. • In Los Angeles, California, artist David Mach is making a sculpture out of 600 Barbie and Ken dolls.

FRIDAY
February 5

The governor of Arizona, Evan Mecham, is impeached by the state's House of Representatives for criminal behavior in office.

SATURDAY
February 6

Happy birthday, President Ronald Reagan, who turns 77 today. • *Good Morning, Vietnam*, starring Robin Williams, is America's top film for the 4th weekend in a row.

SUNDAY
February 7

SKI, D.C, SKI! Part of 19th Street in Washington, D.C., is covered with artificial snow so that people can toboggan and ski on it.

MONDAY
February 8

The International Toy Fair opens in New York City. Toy companies introduce about 5,000 new toys, including a robot that eats spaghetti.

1988: CHINESE YEAR OF THE DRAGON
February 17, 1988–February 5, 1989

According to legend, Buddha summoned all the animals in the world to him one New Year, promising them a reward. Only 12 obeyed, and he gave them each a year; the Rat arrived first, so he got the first year! The order is always the same: Rat, Ox, Tiger, Hare, Dragon, Snake, Horse, Sheep, Monkey, Rooster, Dog, and Pig. In 1988, anyone born before February 17 is a Hare; anyone born on or after February 17 is a Dragon.

People born in the year of the Dragon are usually healthy, generous, enthusiastic, and energetic, but they lose their tempers easily and can be a bit stubborn. They often enjoy being alone. Dragons are very intelligent; they may be perfectionists who ask a lot of other people and themselves. Dragons get along well with Rats, Snakes, Roosters, and Monkeys but *not* with Tigers or Dogs.

Some famous Dragons: Joan of Arc, Sigmund Freud, Sarah Bernhardt, Salvador Dali, Booker T. Washington, Maurice Sendak, Florence Nightingale, Helen Keller, Keanu Reeves, and Dr. Seuss.

TUESDAY
February 9

In the biggest art theft in New York City's history, 18 paintings and 10 drawings worth $6,000,000 are stolen from an art gallery. The 2 thieves broke through a skylight and slid down a rope to enter.
• A dog named Ch. Great Elms Prince Charming II (Prince for short) wins the top prize at the Westminster Kennel Club Show.

WEDNESDAY
February 10

A new exhibit, featuring giant pandas on loan from China, opens at the Calgary Zoo in Canada. • An airplane carrying 65 passengers skids off a runway during a snowstorm at O'Hare International Airport in Chicago, Illinois.

THURSDAY
February 11

An earthquake measuring 4.7 on the Richter scale knocks out the electricity of 29,000 residents in the area of Whittier, California. • Boy Scouts of America votes that women can become Boy Scout leaders.

FRIDAY
February 12

Lincoln's birthday • 2 Soviet warships bump 2 U.S. warships in an area of the Black Sea that the Soviets say is their territory. The U.S. claims the vessels are in international waters.

WHO ELSE WAS BORN IN FEBRUARY?
SUSAN B. ANTHONY

U.S. social reformer
Best known as a leader in the fight for women's rights,
she was president of the National American Woman
Suffrage Association from 1892 to 1900. She was
named to the Hall of Fame for Great Americans in 1950.
BORN   February 15, 1820, in Adams, Massachusetts

SATURDAY
February 13

The Olympic torch arrives in the Canadian city of
Calgary after traveling 11,222 miles from Greece
(5,088 by foot, 4,419 by aircraft and ferry, 1,712
by snowmobile, and 3 by dogsled). The Winter Olympics
officially begin with the lighting of the Olympic flame.

SUNDAY
February 14

Valentine's Day • 61-year-old Cammie Brewer wins a
whopping $6,814,823.48 playing a slot machine (also called a
one-armed bandit) in Reno, Nevada! It's the world's biggest
slot-machine jackpot ever.

MONDAY
February 15

At the Great American Chocolate Festival in Hershey Park,
Pennsylvania, a chocolate bar 7.4 feet long and weighing 1 ton
is displayed, to the delight of chocolate lovers.

TUESDAY
February 16

Julie Koneche of Bemidji, Minnesota, wins the annual Pillsbury
Bake-Off with a delicious praline layer cake. • Gypsy moths
are invading Shenandoah National Park in Virginia!

WEDNESDAY
February 17

New York City's Empire State Building Run-Up,
a race up 86 floors of stairs, is won by Craig Logan
of Australia with a time of 11 minutes, 29 seconds.
Janine Aiello from San Francisco, California, wins the
women's race in 13 minutes, 43 seconds.

THURSDAY
February 18

2,000 Twinkies are given away free to people in Tallahassee,
Florida, who had complained that the snack cake wasn't
available in their town.

FUN FACT '88

Every living thing on earth is descended from a bacterium that lived
in near-boiling water.

THE XV WINTER OLYMPICS
February 13–February 28

The first Winter Olympics were held in France in 1924. Since then, they have been held in different places all over the world. This year, for the first time, they are in Canada. The host city is Calgary—often known as Cow City. 1,700 athletes from 58 countries compete. The official Olympic souvenir is a bear called Howdy. Howdy wears a white cowboy hat and a jacket embroidered with the 5 Olympic rings and a snowflake, which is the logo for this year's games.

THE TOP 5 WINNERS

Soviet Union	29 medals:	11 gold, 9 silver, 9 bronze
East Germany	25 medals:	9 gold, 10 silver, 6 bronze
Switzerland	15 medals:	5 gold, 5 silver, 5 bronze
Austria	10 medals:	3 gold, 5 silver, 2 bronze
West Germany	7 medals:	4 gold, 3 bronze

FRIDAY
February 19

The movie *The Wizard of Oz* is shown for the first time in the Soviet Union. • Fossils discovered in Israel reveal that modern-looking humans were living 92,000 years ago, much earlier than scientists had thought.

SATURDAY
February 20

In a zoo in Holland, twin golden lion tamarins called Matina and Geeles are born. This kind of bright red dwarf monkey from Brazil is almost extinct.

SUNDAY
February 21

A German shepherd named Ulmer wins the annual truffle-sniffing contest in France. Ulmer digs up 6 truffles in 1 minute, 22 seconds.

MONDAY
February 22

Washington's birthday • The Russian world chess champion Gary Kasparov plays 59 simultaneous chess matches with New York City schoolchildren. He wins 57, and 2 are draws.

TUESDAY
February 23

Dinosaur experts report that a 150,000,000-year-old fossil egg found in Utah last September has a dinosaur embryo inside! It may be the oldest dinosaur embryo ever found. From the X-ray pictures, it looks like a tadpole.

SUPERMAN TURNS 50

Superman was created by 2 teenage boys, Jerry Siegel and Joe Shuster, in 1933. Jerry wrote the story for a comic book, and Joe drew the illustrations. It took them 5 years to find someone to publish their comic, but in 1938 Action Comics printed the first *Superman* and it was immediately a big hit.

In 1988, to celebrate Superman's 50th birthday, there is a Superman TV special, a Superman exhibit at the Smithsonian Institution, a Superman cover story in *Time* magazine, and even a new line of clothing: the Krypton Clothing Collection!

WEDNESDAY
February 24

Opera singer Luciano Pavarotti receives 165 curtain calls—the most anyone has ever gotten—after performing at the opera house in Berlin, West Germany.

THURSDAY
February 25

India successfully test-launches its first surface-to-surface missile. • In Industry, California, officials finish cleaning up 38 tons of coins that spilled onto a freeway when an armored truck overturned.

FRIDAY
February 26

SCHOOL'S OUT: 5,000 public schoolteachers go on strike in Cleveland, Ohio. Classes for 73,000 students are canceled.

SATURDAY
February 27

A Gulfstream IV jet sets a new round-the-world speed record when it lands in Houston, Texas, after a flight of 36 hours, 8 minutes. This breaks the record set on January 31.

SUNDAY
February 28

Official closing ceremony of the Winter Olympics in Canada. • Near El Centro, California, 6 earthquakes rock part of the California-Mexico border for 3 hours.

MONDAY
February 29

Leap Year's Day and Superman's 50th birthday • Iran and Iraq bomb each other's capital cities.

KERMIT THE FROG ATTENDS NEWS CONFERENCE IN WASHINGTON, D.C.

HIPPO ATTACKS BICYCLIST IN NAIROBI

GENERAL NORIEGA OF PANAMA IS CHARGED WITH DRUG TRAFFICKING

U.S. MARINE KIDNAPPED IN LEBANON

March

*M*arch is named for the Roman god of war, Mars.

BIRTHSTONE *Aquamarine*

TUESDAY
March 1

Experts in Egypt begin repair work on the famous Sphinx. A piece of its shoulder has fallen off.

WEDNESDAY
March 2

In Venezuela, Michel Menin defies death by walking on a tightrope across Angel Falls. It's 3,304 feet down, the greatest drop over which anyone has walked on a tightrope.

THURSDAY
March 3
Full Moon

A reptile breeder named Albert Kilian goes to the hospital after being bitten by his own rattlesnake in Stamford, Connecticut. • Dr. Seuss is 84 years old today.

FRIDAY
March 4

BRIGHT IDEA: An electronically lit fishing lure has been invented by Michael Garr of Jericho, New York. It's battery operated.

SATURDAY
March 5

A rare, large-footed bird from Indonesia called a maleo hatches at a wildlife center on Saint Catherines Island in Georgia.

SUNDAY
March 6

In New York, Julie Krone becomes the top female jockey in the U.S. when she wins her 1,205th race, riding a horse named Squawter.

MONDAY
March 7

National Procrastination Week begins. • 2,500 TV writers go on strike. They want more royalties and creative rights.

TUESDAY
March 8

A pit bull bites an ear off a boy named Chris Graham in Wilmington, North Carolina. The ear is retrieved from the dog's stomach and successfully reattached to the boy.

WEDNESDAY
March 9

On this day in 1961, a dog named Chernushka (Blackie, in English) became the first dog passenger on a spacecraft, the Soviet Union's *Sputnik 9*.

THURSDAY
March 10

Dr. Howard Hughes and Jacob Kissinger of Hershey, Pennsylvania, have patented a way to make artificial blood vessels.

WHO ELSE WAS BORN IN MARCH?
VINCENT VAN GOGH

Dutch painter
Van Gogh is famous for his Postimpressionist paintings, in which he used thick brushwork and brilliant colors. He suffered from fits of insanity and once even cut off his ear and sent it to someone as a present.
BORN   March 30, 1853, in Zindert, the Netherlands

FRIDAY
March 11

3 men from Great Britain—Sir Ranulph Fiennes, Oliver Shepard, and Dr. Mike Stroud—set off from Ward Hunt Island to walk across the frozen Arctic Ocean to the North Pole, with no dogs or aircraft to help them.

SATURDAY
March 12

The Little League Baseball organization announces that teams in the Soviet Union will be joining the league next year. • Hailstorm in Katmandu, Nepal.

SUNDAY
March 13

The world's longest tunnel opens today—the Seikan Rail Tunnel in Japan. It's 33.5 miles long and links the islands of Hokkaido and Honshu. It has the world's first undersea railway stations—400 feet below sea level.

MONDAY
March 14

The largest cheese in the world is made in Little Chute, Wisconsin. It's cheddar and weighs 40,060 pounds!

TUESDAY
March 15

NASA announces that the ozone layer is disappearing in earth's Northern Hemisphere much faster than expected. Ozone in the atmosphere blocks harmful ultraviolet radiation from the sun.

WEDNESDAY
March 16

Susan Butcher wins the 1,158-mile Iditarod Sled Dog Race in Alaska, beating 53 other sleds. She made it from Anchorage to Nome in 11 days, 11 hours, and 42 minutes.

THURSDAY
March 17

St. Patrick's Day • British scientists have found the remains of a new species of dinosaur in the Sahara Desert. It's a huge, herbivorous sauropod up to 65 feet long.

FUN FACT '88
The favorite color for high-top sneakers in the U.S. is black.

RAIN FOREST COMES TO U.S.

In March 1988, the San Diego Zoo in California opens a spectacular new outdoor exhibit, a simulation of an Asian rain forest, called Tiger River. The exhibit covers 3 acres and contains about 100 animals as well as 5,000 exotic plants. This very realistic re-creation is even misty, just as an actual jungle would be! The mist is made by 300 high-pressure water nozzles hidden throughout the forest.

The inhabitants of Tiger River include 6 Sumatran tigers, which are the world's smallest and rarest tigers; some Malayan tapirs, horselike animals with long noses; and Asian fishing cats, which live in marshes and can catch fish with their paws!

The real rain forests in Africa, Asia, and South America are rapidly being destroyed by pollution and industry. Because tropical rain forests have a huge number of different plants in them, many people are worried about these plants becoming extinct. Experts think that—if nothing is done to stop the destruction of the forests—about 700 plant species will be gone from the planet forever by the year 2000.

FRIDAY
March 18

The European Space Agency and NASA agree to build the first international space station. It will go into orbit in the late 1990s.

SATURDAY
March 19

Huge swarms of desert locusts are spotted on the border of Tunisia and Libya in North Africa.

SUNDAY
March 20

Spring equinox • 8-year-old DeAndra Anrig is lifted 10 feet in the air when her kite gets tangled in the propeller of a small plane flying over Palo Alto, California. She is carried 200 feet—right over her father's head and almost into a tree—before she lets go.

MONDAY
March 21

The annual Rotten Sneakers Contest, held in Montpelier, Vermont, is won by Bob Scruten, age 8. The contest (which is broadcast on TV) is based on the condition of the shoe's heel, sole, and tongue—and on its odor!

TUESDAY
March 22

The U.S. Fish and Wildlife Service ships 2 Alaskan musk oxen to a new home in the Beijing Zoo in China. Their names are Koyuk and Tanana.

WEDNESDAY
March 23

Butterfly World in Coconut Creek, Florida, opens. It has between 2,000 and 3,000 butterflies and cost $1,500,000 to build.

THURSDAY
March 24

The Soviet Union launches a spacecraft to carry supplies to 2 cosmonauts on the space station *Mir*. They have been there since last December.
• In Indianapolis, Indiana, Mellissa Sanders comes down from the top of a 43-foot-high pole, where she has stayed for 517 days to set a world record in pole-sitting.

FRIDAY
March 25

Robbers hold up an armored truck in Brooklyn, New York, while 2 of the 3 guards are eating lunch. The thieves escape with over $1,200,000 in cash. • Sir Ranulph Fiennes and his team give up their expedition (begun on March 11) because of frostbite.

SATURDAY
March 26

The San Diego Zoo in California opens the Tiger River exhibit, a replica of a rain forest in Asia.

SUNDAY
March 27

An animal-rights group steals 73 rabbits from a rabbit-breeding company in Haywood, California. The group doesn't want the rabbits used for medical research or for food.

MONDAY
March 28

30 coats of old paint are being carefully removed, using chemicals, from the outside of the White House. It's part of a project to restore and repair the presidential home.

TUESDAY
March 29

British bomb-disposal experts detonate a 2,000-pound World War II German torpedo after it gets caught in fishing nets off the coast of England.

WEDNESDAY
March 30

On this day in 1867, the U.S. bought Alaska from the Russians for $7,200,000.

THURSDAY
March 31

In the largest international drug bust in history, the United States and Italy arrest 233 people (69 in the U.S.) suspected of being part of a drug ring in which heroin was traded for cocaine.

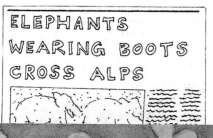

ELEPHANTS WEARING BOOTS CROSS ALPS

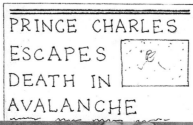

PRINCE CHARLES ESCAPES DEATH IN AVALANCHE

SOVIET CREDIT CARD LAUNCHED

April

*T*he name April comes from the Latin *aperire*, which means "to open." April is known as the time of budding.

BIRTHSTONE *Diamond*

FRIDAY
April 1

April Fools' Day • Good Friday • Passover begins at sundown. • A man named René Bricka sets off from the Canary Islands to walk across the Atlantic Ocean on a pair of 14-foot-long polyester floats.

SATURDAY
April 2
Full Moon

9-year-old Tony Aliengena lands his plane in Bedford, Massachusetts, becoming the youngest pilot to cross the U.S. He left San Juan Capistrano, California, 4 days ago.

SUNDAY
April 3

Easter • Chop Chop the pig becomes surfing champ at the "Wet Pet" Surfing Championships in Honolulu, Hawaii.

MONDAY
April 4

The University of Kansas beats the University of Oklahoma, 83–79, in the NCAA basketball championship.

TUESDAY
April 5

A man fishing near Kennedy Airport in New York catches a bag full of bonds worth $5,000,000.
• In Indianapolis, Indiana, the world's tallest woman is honored. Sandy Allen is 7 feet, 7¼ inches tall.

IT'S A . . . BABY CONDOR!

The first California condor to be conceived in captivity is hatched at the San Diego Wild Animal Park. Only 27 others exist, all in captivity.

The egg, which is 5 inches long and weighs 10 ounces, is kept in an incubator for 55 days. On April 27, the first crack appears in the shell, as the condor begins to peck from inside. By the end of the day, there is a dime-sized hole. On April 29, zookeepers use tiny tweezers to help the baby break out of its shell, ending the 61½-hour hatching.

The new arrival is named Molloko, which is a Native American word for condor. It is yellow and has a bald head. Molloko is placed in the type of incubator used for premature human babies, and on April 30 is given its first meal: minced mice!

WHO ELSE WAS BORN IN APRIL?
ULYSSES S. GRANT

18th president of the United States (1869–1877)
A general and a national hero, he led the Union
Army to victory in the Civil War.

BORN   April 27, 1822, in Point Pleasant, Ohio

WEDNESDAY
April 6

The 10,000th McDonald's restaurant
opens in Dale City, Virginia.

THURSDAY
April 7

International No-Smoking Day. In New York City, smoking is
banned from all public places for today; in Nepal, the king
orders all cigarette factories to shut down for 2 hours; and in
Beijing, there are fines for lighting up!

FRIDAY
April 8

U.S. and Canadian dinosaur experts have found a new
dinosaur, a pygmy tyrannosaur called Nanotyrannus. It was
about a third as long as the giant Tyrannosaurus rex. The
discovery comes from a skull that was wrongly identified 60
years ago.

SATURDAY
April 9

The owner of an exotic pet shop in West Haven, Connecticut,
discovers that burglars have stolen $8,000 worth of pets,
including 35 tarantulas, 32 snakes, 12 scorpions, and 8 iguanas.

SUNDAY
April 10

For the first time in 7 years, *Sesame Street* is shown on television
in Japan. Adults are watching it to improve their English.

MONDAY
April 11

Researchers at Harvard University in Massachusetts receive a
patent for their genetically altered mouse. This is the
world's first patent for an animal.

TUESDAY
April 12

American pizza is sold in the Soviet Union for the
first time. People line up in the snow to buy it from
a van; 1,200 slices are sold in the first 3 hours!

WEDNESDAY
April 13

CHOCOLATE MELTDOWN: In Newstead, New York,
a truck full of chocolate bars and caramel catches
fire on the highway and melts into a gooey mess.

FUN FACT '88
More than 1 billion Easter eggs are dyed this year. Favorite color: pink.

DAEDALUS SETS 3 RECORDS

On April 23, Greek cycling champion Kanellos Kanellopoulos crosses the Aegean Sea from Crete to Santorini in a plane powered by foot pedals. It takes him 3 hours, 54 minutes, to travel the 74 miles between the islands. His speed is about 18 miles per hour, and he flies only 15 feet above the water.

The aircraft is called the *Daedalus 88*, named after the mythical figure who escaped from Crete with wings made of wax and feathers. The ultralight plane is pink and silver, with a wingspan of 112 feet. It weighs 72 pounds.

The *Daedalus 88* sets 3 new world records:
1. Distance record for human-powered flight of any kind
2. Distance record for human-powered straight-line flight
3. Duration record for human-powered flight (time in the air)

THURSDAY
April 14

In a special ceremony in Washington, D.C., President Reagan gives Terry Weeks a crystal apple for winning the National Teacher of the Year Award.

FRIDAY
April 15

Using telescopes on Hawaii's Mauna Kea volcano, astronomers have detected a galaxy almost twice as far away from earth as any found before.

SATURDAY
April 16

500 fire fighters battle 90 wildfires in Minnesota. About 90,000 acres of grass and woods in the state have already burned.

SUNDAY
April 17

BICYCLES GALORE: 1,816,300 people participate in a huge bicycle parade in San Juan, Puerto Rico.

MONDAY
April 18

The Boston Marathon is won by Ibrahim Hussein of Kenya with a time of 2 hours, 8 minutes, 43 seconds. The women's race is won by Rosa Mota of Portugal; her time is 2 hours, 24 minutes, 30 seconds.

TUESDAY
April 19

At Sotheby's in New York City, Laurence Graff of Great Britain buys a flawless egg-sized, pear-shaped 85.91-carat diamond for the record price of $9,130,000.

WEDNESDAY
April 20

In Altoona, Wisconsin, schoolteacher Alice Meyer uses mouth-to-mouth resuscitation to save a pupil's 2-week-old puppy, which was suffocating in a book bag.

THURSDAY
April 21

French archaeologists have found a pair of 4,000-year-old pyramids beneath the desert sand near Cairo, Egypt.

FRIDAY
April 22

Earth Day • B.J. Watkins is rescued 500 miles north of Bermuda in her wrecked boat, the *Heart*. She was on her way to England, sailing alone, when the steering malfunctioned and the mast broke.

SATURDAY
April 23

RECORD-BREAKING FLIGHT: Kanellos Kanellopoulos flies a human-powered aircraft 74 miles between the Greek islands of Crete and Santorini.

SUNDAY
April 24

At an auction in New York City, a collection of cookie jars that had belonged to artist Andy Warhol sells for $247,000.

MONDAY
April 25

A new Coast Guard plane designed to spot and track drug dealers' planes is unveiled in Washington, D.C. It's equipped with the latest radar and infrared systems.

TUESDAY
April 26

A 40,000,000-year-old piece of hair has been found in the Caribbean! It is preserved in amber and proves that there were land mammals in the area at that time.

WEDNESDAY
April 27

A rare California condor chick starts to peck its way out of its egg at the San Diego Wild Animal Park. Zookeepers play recorded vulture noises to encourage the chick.

THURSDAY
April 28

On a flight from Hilo to Honolulu in Hawaii, a 20-foot gaping hole suddenly opens in the cabin of a jet. The plane manages to land safely on Maui.

FRIDAY
April 29

The first California condor conceived in captivity is hatched in San Diego, California. • McDonald's makes a deal with the Soviet Union to open 20 McDonald's restaurants in Moscow. The Big Mac will be called the Bolshoi and will sell for 2 rubles.

SATURDAY
April 30

The longest banana split in the world is made in Selinsgrove, Pennsylvania. It is 4.55 miles long!

STEEL WORKERS STRIKE IN POLAND

11,200-YEAR-OLD CLOVIS SPEAR POINT FOUND

KILLER TORNADO SWEEPS THROUGH FLORIDA

2,500 GOATS STOLEN IN KENYA

May

May comes from Maia, who was the Roman goddess of growth, increase, and blossoming.

BIRTHSTONE *Emerald*

SUNDAY
May 1
Full Moon

4 women leave New York City today to re-create the first women's motorcycle ride across the U.S., made in 1966 by Augusta and Adelaide Van Buren. They will arrive in Los Angeles in a month. • Dust storm near Selbert, Colorado.

MONDAY
May 2

$1,000 in quarters spills from a truck onto a highway in Boston, Massachusetts. Someone in a passing car gets out, picks up coins worth $100, and scrams!

TUESDAY
May 3

Doctors in South Africa successfully separate 16-month-old Siamese twin girls who were joined at the head. The operation takes 7½ hours.

WEDNESDAY
May 4

The largest topaz in the world, a 5⅞-inch-wide, 22,892.5-carat gem with 172 facets, goes on display at the Smithsonian Institution in Washington, D.C. • In Nevada, a factory that makes fuel for space shuttles explodes.

THURSDAY
May 5

Mountain climbers from China, Japan, and Nepal take part in the first live TV broadcast from the top of Mount Everest, commemorating the first successful climb 35 years ago.

FRIDAY
May 6

A chocolate company in Switzerland has invented a kind of chocolate that won't melt in hot weather—though it will still melt in your mouth!

SATURDAY
May 7

In Louisville, Kentucky, the Kentucky Derby is won by a horse named Winning Colors, which wins by a neck.

SUNDAY
May 8

Mother's Day • 81 tornadoes are reported in Illinois, Wisconsin, Iowa, Indiana, and Arkansas.

MOON FLASH

On May 31, there is a blue moon! The moon isn't *really* blue, though. Whenever there are 2 full moons in a month, the 2d is always called a blue moon. The last blue moon was in July 1985.

WHO ELSE WAS BORN IN MAY?
MARTHA GRAHAM

U.S. dancer and choreographer
A major pioneer of modern dance, she
choreographed more than 100 works. In 1976,
she was awarded the U.S. Medal of Freedom.
BORN   May 11, 1893, in Pittsburgh, Pennsylvania

MONDAY
May 9

3-year-old Prince Henry of England
has a hernia operation in London.

TUESDAY
May 10

Record holders from the *Guinness Book of World Records* meet at
a convention in New York City, including the world's fastest
talker, a person who plays the world's smallest violin, the
world's best underwater pogo-stick jumper, and the world's
youngest karate black belt (age 8).

WEDNESDAY
May 11

9-year-old Bridgette Ellis becomes the youngest person to fly
solo. She flies in a homemade aircraft for 3 minutes near
Montgomery, Illinois.

THURSDAY
May 12

Stephen Venables of Great Britain climbs the
east face of Mount Everest without the use
of oxygen, a feat never accomplished before.

FRIDAY
May 13

A 460-pound silverback gorilla named Willie B. leaves his
indoor cell and goes outside for the first time in 27 years, at a
new exhibit at Zoo Atlanta in Georgia.

SATURDAY
May 14

Brownie Troop 807 from Corpus Christi, Texas, has sent 402
boxes of Girl Scout cookies to sailors on board the USS
Midway, stationed in Japan.

SUNDAY
May 15

180 former soda jerks get free hot fudge sundaes at the
National Soda Jerk Reunion in Omaha, Nebraska. (A soda jerk
is someone who works at a soda fountain.)

FUN FACT '88

The hairstreak butterfly has fake antennae on the back of its wings
to fool birds, which kill butterflies by pecking them on the head.

1988 AWARDS BOARD

Nobel Peace Prize: United Nations Peacekeeping Forces
National Teacher of the Year: Terry Weeks of Murfreesboro, Tennessee
National Spelling Bee Champion: Rageshree Ramanchandran of Fair Oaks, California
Female Athlete of the Year: Florence Griffith Joyner, track
Male Athlete of the Year: Orel Hershiser, baseball
Horse of the Year: Alysheba
Best Movie (Academy Award): *Rain Man*
Best Special/Visual Effects (Academy Award): *Who Framed Roger Rabbit?*
Best Album (Grammy Award): George Michael, *Faith*
Best Single (Grammy Award): Bobby McFerrin, "Don't Worry, Be Happy"
Best children's book (Newbery Medal): *Lincoln: A Photobiography* by Russell Freedman
Best children's book illustration (Caldecott Medal): *Owl Moon* by Jane Yolen, illustrated by John Schoenherr.

MONDAY
May 16

The U.S. Surgeon General announces that cigarettes are as addictive as drugs and alcohol. • A man in New Jersey has invented chewing gum candy!

TUESDAY
May 17

The first ad for Pepsi is shown on television in the Soviet Union; it features Michael Jackson singing and dancing.

WEDNESDAY
May 18

7 black-footed ferrets are born in Sybille Canyon, Wyoming. The births bring the total world population of this endangered species to 38.

THURSDAY
May 19

Over 600 frogs from around the world enter the jumping contest at the Calaveras County Jumping Frog Jubilee in California.

FRIDAY
May 20

In the Netherlands, thieves smash windows at an Amsterdam museum and steal 3 paintings worth $52,000,000. • At Busch Gardens in Williamsburg, Virginia, 13 roller-coaster lovers ride the Loch Ness Monster for 10 hours!

SATURDAY
May 21

A horse named Risen Star wins the Preakness in Baltimore, Maryland. • Large clumps of reddish brown jelly, an alga called *Chrysocyhromulina polylepsis*, ooze along the coasts of Denmark and Sweden, killing the fish.

SUNDAY *May 22*	On this day in 1892, the toothpaste tube was invented by Dr. Washington Sheffield.
MONDAY *May 23*	Researchers at Cornell University have found out that some female moths spray a kind of perfume out of their stomachs to attract the opposite sex.
TUESDAY *May 24*	3 window washers are saved by the fire department in Charlotte, North Carolina, after their scaffolding collapses. Rescuers found the 3 dangling outside the 18th floor of a high rise.
WEDNESDAY *May 25*	HOLD ON, MITZIE! Bob Halgreen and his dog, Mitzie, have broken the world record for man and dog traveling on a motorcycle. They've just reached their 24th state: Idaho.
THURSDAY *May 26*	The Edmonton Oilers win the National Hockey League's Stanley Cup for the 4th time in 5 years.
FRIDAY *May 27*	Australia's Kay Cottee rounds the tip of southern Tasmania on her 181st day at sea. She is trying to become the first woman to sail around the world alone and nonstop.
SATURDAY *May 28*	The world's first on-line computer marriage takes place between Rose Anne Detrafford and Joe Malacria. The ceremony is held on a New York City electronic bulletin board.
SUNDAY *May 29*	In Indiana, the Indianapolis 500 auto race is won by Rick Mears. Average speed: 114.809 miles per hour.
MONDAY *May 30*	Memorial Day • In Moscow: President Reagan, on his first visit to the Soviet Union, calls for that country to pay more attention to human rights.
TUESDAY *May 31* Full Moon (Blue Moon)	Dutch police report the recovery of the 3 paintings worth $52,000,000 that were stolen on May 20. They arrested 3 men trying to sell the works of art in a hotel.

SIBERIAN TIGER KILLS ZOOKEEPER IN HOUSTON, TEXAS

SCIENTISTS SAY THE SUN HAS THROWN OUT A PIECE OF ITSELF.

3 FRENCH HOSTAGES FREED IN BEIRUT, LEBANON

NEWSWEEK REPORTS FIRST LADY USES ASTROLOGER TO PLAN PRESIDENT'S DAY

June

*J*une is named for the Latin *juniores*, meaning "youths," or from the goddess Juno.

BIRTHSTONE *Pearl*

WEDNESDAY
June 1

In Hollywood, California, Universal Studio Tours opens a new attraction: Star Trek Adventure. Visitors can act in a special *Star Trek* "episode," with authentic sets and props.

THURSDAY
June 2

A 13-year-old girl from Fair Oaks, California, Rageshree Ramanchandran, wins the Scripps-Howard National Spelling Bee in Washington, D.C. Winning word: elegiacal.

FRIDAY
June 3

DUCK LUCK: In Papillion, Nebraska, a mother duck—with 17 baby ducklings following obediently behind—crosses a busy street and runs over a sewer grate. The mother waddles on, but the ducklings are so small they fall through the grate! Townspeople save the ducklings, which are taken to a nearby zoo.

SATURDAY
June 4

René Bricka, who set out April 1 (wearing huge floats on his feet) to walk across the Atlantic Ocean, arrives in Trinidad.
• 84,358 people in 94 countries play bridge, in the world's largest card game. Jan Horowitz and Barbara Norante win, playing in Paris, France.

SUNDAY
June 5

Kay Cottee arrives in Sydney, Australia, and becomes the first woman to sail alone nonstop around the world. She left on November 29, 1987.

MONDAY
June 6

Great Britain's Per Lindstrom sets an altitude record (64,996 feet) in Laredo, Texas, in his 12-story-high hot-air balloon, the *Stratoquest*. He has to climb out of the capsule at 22,000 feet to cut off 2 sandbags with a knife!

TUESDAY
June 7

1 Bulgarian and 2 Soviet cosmonauts take off in a *Soyuz* spacecraft on a 10-day mission to the orbiting *Mir* space station.

WHO ELSE WAS BORN IN JUNE?
BABE DIDRIKSON ZAHARIAS

U.S. athlete
An all-around athlete, she was an All-American basketball player who also won gold medals and set records at the 1932 Olympics for javelin and 80-meter hurdles. She won the U.S. Open golf championship in 1948, 1950, and 1954, and was named Associated Press Woman Athlete of the Century in 1950.

BORN June 26, 1914, in Port Arthur, Texas

WEDNESDAY
June 8
The House of Representatives passes a law limiting the number of commercials allowed in children's TV programs.

THURSDAY
June 9
In Czechoslovakia, Soviet pole-vaulter Sergei Bubka breaks his own world record with a mighty vault of 19 feet, 10½ inches.

FRIDAY
June 10
HOP TO IT! 14 members of the senior class at Hanover High School in Hanover, New Hampshire, begin leapfrogging to try to break the world record.

SATURDAY
June 11

11-year-old Adragon Eastwood De Mello graduates from the University of California in Santa Cruz, California, with a B.A. in mathematics.
• Risen Star wins the Belmont Stakes horse race—by an amazing 14¾ lengths!

SUNDAY
June 12
U.S. officials have seized several million dollars' worth of illegal fireworks—spinners, cherry balls, and Roman candles—from ports up and down the East Coast.

MONDAY
June 13
A team of 32 divers begin taking turns pedaling a tricycle underwater in Santa Barbara, California, to raise money for the Muscular Dystrophy Association.

FUN FACT '88

In an average lifetime, a person will spend 5 years waiting in lines and 6 years eating.

TOP TEN NAMES FOR BABIES IN 1988

	BOYS				GIRLS	
1	Michael	6	Justin	1 Ashley	6	Jennifer
2	Matthew	7	Daniel	2 Jessica	7	Katherine
3	Christopher	8	Ryan	3 Amanda	8	Rachel
4	Joshua	9	James	4 Sarah	9	Stephanie
5	Andrew	10	David	5 Megan	10	Heather

TUESDAY
June 14

Gold and silver treasure from 2 shipwrecks is auctioned in New York City for $2,580,000. It was found off the coast of Florida by treasure hunter Mel Fisher.

WEDNESDAY
June 15

BIG CHEESE: The world's biggest piece of cheese, 40,060 pounds of cheddar, makes its first stop on a 36-city tour: Los Angeles. The cheese is driven around town in a glass-walled, climate-controlled truck and is chased by people dressed as mice!

THURSDAY
June 16

The underwater tricyclers who began on Monday stop today. They have pedaled 116.66 miles.

FRIDAY
June 17

5 fishermen arrive in Honolulu, Hawaii, after 5 months spent drifting in the Pacific Ocean on a floundering boat. They lived on rainwater, turtles, and fish until they were rescued by a Japanese fishing boat.

SATURDAY
June 18

In New Hampshire, the Hanover leapfroggers who began June 10 break the leapfrogging world record—they've gone 888.1 miles! • 600 llama lovers meet at the International Llama Association's conference in Bellaire, Michigan.

SUNDAY
June 19

Father's Day • In Brooklyn, New York, 4 people happen to be passing by just in time to catch a woman who dives headfirst out of her burning 3d-floor apartment. They also catch her boyfriend, who leaps feetfirst.

MONDAY
June 20

Summer solstice • Curtis Strange wins the U.S. Open golf tournament in Brookline, Massachusetts.

TUESDAY
June 21

The NBA basketball championship is won by the Los Angeles Lakers, who defeat the Detroit Pistons. • A pair of ruby slippers worn by Dorothy (Judy Garland) in *The Wizard of Oz* are sold for $165,000 in New York City.

WEDNESDAY *June 22*	The new movie *Who Framed Roger Rabbit?* opens today across the U.S. It has both animated (cartoon) and live characters in it.
THURSDAY *June 23*	13-year-old Shannon Catasso of Allegheny County, Pennsylvania, wins the 65th annual Marble Tournament in Wildwood, New Jersey. The prize is a $2,000 scholarship.
FRIDAY *June 24*	Dredges are working around the clock in St. Louis, Missouri, to clear sandbars in the Mississippi River. The driest spring in 50 years has left the water level so low that boats are getting stuck!
SATURDAY *June 25*	National Fink Day in Fink, Texas, featuring the Fink Olympics, with a Ping-Pong shot putting event. • Annual Rooster Crow in Rogue River, Oregon.
SUNDAY *June 26*	Great Britain's Dave Hurst and Alan Matthews become the first blind men to climb Mont Blanc, the highest mountain in Europe.
MONDAY *June 27*	Skyscrapers sway in San Francisco, California, during an earthquake measuring 5.1 on the Richter scale. It's the 3d quake in 2 days.
TUESDAY *June 28*	A painting by Claude Monet is bought at a London auction for $24,590,000, the highest price ever paid for an impressionist work.
WEDNESDAY *June 29* Full Moon	A new species of fish has been captured 8,000 feet (about 1½ miles) under the Pacific Ocean off the Galápagos Islands. It's 12 inches long, with a large head and a small mouth with teeth.
THURSDAY *June 30*	According to NASA scientists, the earth is heating up due to the greenhouse effect. The first half of 1988 has been warmer than any year since records were kept.

WHO FRAMED ROGER RABBIT? BREAKS BOX OFFICE RECORDS

2,000,000 BLACK SOUTH AFRICANS STRIKE

BATMOBILE SOLD FOR $180,000

VALENTINE'S DAY CARD MAILED 45 YEARS AGO FINALLY DELIVERED

July

This month was named to honor Julius Caesar.

FRIDAY
July 1

At an auction in Kennebunk, Maine, a handmade copper fishing lure from 1859 is sold for $22,000! • Happy 27th birthday to Diana, the Princess of Wales.

SATURDAY
July 2

Steffi Graf wins the women's singles Wimbledon tennis championship. • Sam Ferrans breaks the World Flying Disk (Frisbee) Federation outdoor distance record with a throw of 623.6 feet in La Habra, California. • In Eau Claire, Michigan, Rick Krause breaks the cherry-pit-spitting record with a spit of 72 feet, 7½ inches.

SUNDAY
July 3

Rocky Kenoyer sets a new world record in skydiving by falling to earth 403 times in 24 hours, at Snohomish, Washington.

MONDAY
July 4

Independence Day • Stefan Edberg beats Boris Becker to win the men's singles tennis championship at Wimbledon in England.

TUESDAY
July 5

Space shuttle *Discovery* has been moved from its 52-story hangar to the launching pad at Cape Canaveral, Florida. Its first flight is scheduled for September.

WEDNESDAY
July 6

A huge explosion destroys an oil platform in the North Sea— it's the worst offshore oil rig disaster in history.

THURSDAY
July 7

The Soviet Union launches an unmanned spacecraft to investigate one of Mars's 2 moons, Phobos (which means "fear"). The craft will come within 165 feet of the moon. • In Philadelphia, Pennsylvania, Antonio Gonzalez wins a contest for the biggest roach with a 2-inch-long cockroach.

FRIDAY
July 8

USA Today reports that the U.S. has more billionaires than any other country: 67.

SATURDAY
July 9

Raymond Houtmans catches a record-breaking 97-pound tigerfish in the Zaire River in Zaire. • 1,500 people play in the World Championship Domino Tournament in Andalusia, Alabama.

WHO ELSE WAS BORN IN JULY?
BEATRIX POTTER

British children's book author
She both wrote and illustrated her books, which are still very popular and include such classics as *The Tale of Peter Rabbit* (1902) and *The Tale of Squirrel Nutkin* (1903).
BORN   July 28, 1866, in South Kensington, Middlesex, England

SUNDAY
July 10

4 people in Riviera, Florida, are arrested for taking 1,088 turtle eggs from the beach. The eggs are from either the endangered green turtle or the threatened loggerhead turtle, and it is illegal to take them.

MONDAY
July 11

Daniel Bakke of North Dakota has invented a device that turns a normal outdoor lamp into an insect electrocution machine.

TUESDAY
July 12

The American League wins baseball's All-Star Game in Cincinnati, Ohio. • The Soviet Union launches a 2d unmanned spacecraft to Mars. Both craft are equipped to explore the Martian moon Phobos.

WEDNESDAY
July 13

More than 1,000 jugglers attend the International Jugglers Association meeting in Denver, Colorado.

THURSDAY
July 14

11-year-old Christopher Marshall lands in Paris, France, after flying his single-engine plane across the U.S. and the Atlantic Ocean, retracing the famous 1927 flight by Charles Lindbergh. The boy, who was accompanied by an adult, left San Diego, California, on July 7.

Is this Los Angeles?

WRONG WAY, GARRISON!

July 17 is the 50th anniversary of Douglas "Wrong Way" Garrison's famous wrong-way flight. In 1938, Garrison took off in his plane from New York to go to California. Some 28 hours later, he landed in Ireland and asked, "Is this Los Angeles?" In 1988, on the anniversary of his mistake, "Wrong Way" celebrates by taking a commercial flight from Los Angeles to New York, en route to Ireland. He carries just $3 in his wallet, as he did in 1938.

WHAT'S HOT IN 1988

Teenage Mutant Ninja Turtles
Nintendo video games
Roger Rabbit
Garfield
The California Raisins
Dinosaurs

Toy kitchens
Denim jeans with holes in the knees
Bozo the clown
Bow ties
L'il Earl the Dead Cat
Teddy Grahams (cookies)

Hottest T-shirt: ALF FOR PRESIDENT
Hottest videos: *Cinderella* and *E.T.: The Extraterrestrial*

FRIDAY
July 15

A giant hot-air balloon shaped like Mickey Mouse's head arrives in Philadelphia, Pennsylvania, as part of Mickey's 60th birthday celebration.

SATURDAY
July 16

Florence Griffith Joyner runs the fastest women's 100-meter race ever in Indianapolis, Indiana—10.49 seconds!

SUNDAY
July 17

U.S. HEAT WAVE: It's the hottest day on record in San Francisco, California: 104°F. It's 102° in Philadelphia, Pennyslvania; 101° in Baltimore, Maryland; and a scorching 114° in Needles, California.

MONDAY
July 18

2 Vietnamese box turtles hatch at the Bronx Zoo in New York City. It's the first known breeding of this rare species in a zoo.

TUESDAY
July 19

6,000 motor homes are brought to South Bend, Indiana, for the 25th convention of the Family Motor Coach Association.

WEDNESDAY
July 20

2 Mediterranean fruit flies are found in Los Angeles, California. They are extremely dangerous to crops.

THURSDAY
July 21

THE FISH ARE BITING: Fish are biting swimmers in Lake Mendocino in California. Officials don't know what kind of fish are making the attacks; some people say Indian spirits are angry because the lake is built on top of a Pomo Indian burial ground!

FRIDAY
July 22

300 bicyclists arrive in Atlantic City, New Jersey, after cycling across the U.S. on the 3,400-mile TransAmerica Bicycle Trek. They left Seattle, Washington, on June 6.

FUN FACT '88

July is National Hot Dog Month. People in the U.S. eat a total of 50,000,000 hot dogs every day.

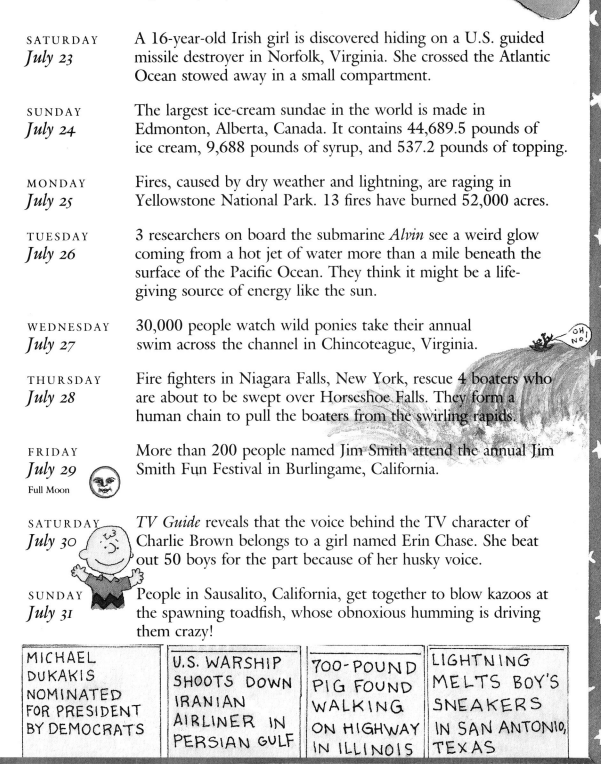

SATURDAY
July 23

A 16-year-old Irish girl is discovered hiding on a U.S. guided missile destroyer in Norfolk, Virginia. She crossed the Atlantic Ocean stowed away in a small compartment.

SUNDAY
July 24

The largest ice-cream sundae in the world is made in Edmonton, Alberta, Canada. It contains 44,689.5 pounds of ice cream, 9,688 pounds of syrup, and 537.2 pounds of topping.

MONDAY
July 25

Fires, caused by dry weather and lightning, are raging in Yellowstone National Park. 13 fires have burned 52,000 acres.

TUESDAY
July 26

3 researchers on board the submarine *Alvin* see a weird glow coming from a hot jet of water more than a mile beneath the surface of the Pacific Ocean. They think it might be a life-giving source of energy like the sun.

WEDNESDAY
July 27

30,000 people watch wild ponies take their annual swim across the channel in Chincoteague, Virginia.

THURSDAY
July 28

Fire fighters in Niagara Falls, New York, rescue 4 boaters who are about to be swept over Horseshoe Falls. They form a human chain to pull the boaters from the swirling rapids.

FRIDAY
July 29
Full Moon

More than 200 people named Jim Smith attend the annual Jim Smith Fun Festival in Burlingame, California.

SATURDAY
July 30

TV Guide reveals that the voice behind the TV character of Charlie Brown belongs to a girl named Erin Chase. She beat out 50 boys for the part because of her husky voice.

SUNDAY
July 31

People in Sausalito, California, get together to blow kazoos at the spawning toadfish, whose obnoxious humming is driving them crazy!

| MICHAEL DUKAKIS NOMINATED FOR PRESIDENT BY DEMOCRATS | U.S. WARSHIP SHOOTS DOWN IRANIAN AIRLINER IN PERSIAN GULF | 700-POUND PIG FOUND WALKING ON HIGHWAY IN ILLINOIS | LIGHTNING MELTS BOY'S SNEAKERS IN SAN ANTONIO, TEXAS |

August

August was named in honor of Roman emperor Augustus, whose lucky month it was.

BIRTHSTONE *Peridot*

MONDAY
August 1

An earthquake measuring 3.7 on the Richter scale shakes the Rockies in Idaho.

TUESDAY
August 2

Skip Storch is on the last leg of his swim down the Hudson River from Albany, New York, to the Statue of Liberty. The 153-mile swim takes him 54 hours, 50 minutes; he does it over an 8-day period.

WEDNESDAY
August 3

Astronomers announce that they have found 10 objects orbiting distant stars—one of the "planets" is 20 times the size of earth and is 522 trillion miles away.

THURSDAY
August 4

Guns belonging to the famous outlaw Jesse James are given to Clay County, Missouri, by his last surviving granddaughter. His pistol, holster, boots, and spurs will be on permanent display so that visitors can see them.

FRIDAY
August 5

2 scientists from Duke University in North Carolina have invented a breathing machine that could allow humans to breathe underwater without the use of an oxygen tank.

SATURDAY
August 6

More than 3,000 twins come to the Twins Day Festival in Twinsburg, Ohio. Twinsburg was founded in 1817 by twins who worked together, got married together, and died on the same day!

SUNDAY
August 7

Great Britain's Harry Taylor and New Zealand's Russell Brice become the first people to successfully climb Mount Everest's northeast ridge.

FUN FACT '88

There are 2 bicycles for every car in the world. In China, there are 540 bicycles for every car!

WHO ELSE WAS BORN IN AUGUST?
ALEX HALEY

U.S. author
He is most famous for *Roots*, his 1976 book about his black heritage, which won a special Pulitzer Prize and was made into a TV miniseries. He also transcribed and organized *The Autobiography of Malcolm X*.
BORN   August 11, 1921, in Ithaca, New York

MONDAY
August 8

In Chicago, Illinois, the Chicago Cubs play the Philadelphia Phillies in the first night game at Wrigley Field, the last ballpark in the U.S. to install lights. The game is rained out.

TUESDAY
August 9

Astronomers have found a galaxy 15 billion light-years away from earth, farther than any found before. It is named 4C41.17.

WEDNESDAY
August 10

Rik Dunkan of Australia hang glides down Mount Fuji, the highest mountain in Japan. It takes him about an hour.

THURSDAY
August 11

President Reagan signs a bill that will give help to farmers and ranchers hurt by the terrible drought affecting much of the U.S.

FRIDAY
August 12

A fire breaks out on the 86th floor of the Empire State Building in New York City. 250 tourists are evacuated.
• Earthquake in Tokyo: 5.3 on the Richter scale.

SATURDAY
August 13

An antique doll, made in Germany about 1910, is sold at an auction in Anaheim, California, for the record high price of $48,000.

SUNDAY
August 14

Peter Purdy of Seattle, Washington, has patented an ultrasonic speedometer for skiers. • Several earthquakes—one of them 5.6 on the Richter scale—shake central Utah.

MONDAY
August 15

There is another fire at the Empire State Building in New York City, the 2d in 4 days. 10 rolls of carpet stored in a stairway start the fire.

TOP TEN SINGLES OF 1988*

1	"So Emotional"	Whitney Houston
2	"Got My Mind Set on You"	George Harrison
3	"The Way You Make Me Feel"	Michael Jackson
4	"Need You Tonight"	INXS
5	"Could've Been"	Tiffany
6	"Seasons Change"	Expose
7	"Father Figure"	George Michael
8	"Never Gonna Give You Up"	Rick Astley
9	"Man in the Mirror"	Michael Jackson
10	"Get outta My Dreams, Get into My Car"	Billy Ocean

*Source: *Billbaord.*

TUESDAY August 16
Chinese and Canadian scientists have found a fossilized cluster of baby ankylosaurs (a kind of dinosaur) that died together 75,000,000 years ago in what is now Inner Mongolia. The grouping shows the dinosaurs may have lived as families.

WEDNESDAY August 17
For the first time in history, U.S. and Soviet scientists conduct a joint nuclear test, setting off a nuclear device 2,000 feet below the Nevada desert.

THURSDAY August 18
Officials at the Walters Art Gallery in Baltimore, Maryland, announce that a clever thief has somehow sneaked out with small Asian artworks worth $500,000.

FRIDAY August 19
In Miami, Florida, David Coburn breaks the record for domino stacking by piling up 291 dominoes on top of a single domino.

SATURDAY August 20
The autumn buttercup, thought to be extinct since 1900, has been found growing along the Sevier River in Utah.

SUNDAY August 21
A very powerful earthquake (6.7 on the Richter scale) rocks the foothills of the Himalayas along the border of India and Nepal.

MONDAY August 22

100 children compete in the double Dutch jump-rope competition—jumping 2 ropes at the same time—at Grand Central Terminal in New York City.

TUESDAY August 23	The Olympic flame is lit at the Temple of Hera at Olympia in Greece. The first of 350 runners starts the torch relay across Greece to Seoul in South Korea for the opening ceremony of the games on September 17.
WEDNESDAY August 24	A guard at the Walters Art Gallery in Baltimore, Maryland, has been arrested for stealing. The FBI and police found 84 missing pieces of art in his basement.
THURSDAY August 25	FIRES STILL RAGING: More than 380,000 acres of trees and grass in Yellowstone National Park have been destroyed by out-of-control wildfires.
FRIDAY August 26	Lynne Cox of the U.S. swims across Lake Baikal in Siberia, where the water temperature is 52°F. It takes her 4 hours, 20 minutes.
SATURDAY August 27 Full Moon	Get ready for this pitch, Hawaii! The team from Taiwan beats the team from Pearl City, Hawaii, in baseball's Little League World Series in Williamsport, Pennsylvania.
SUNDAY August 28	Escape artist Anthony Martin is placed in handcuffs and chains, locked inside a box, and then thrown out of a plane. He emerges at 7,500 feet and parachutes to safety near Sandwich, Illinois.
MONDAY August 29	An Afghan-Soviet space mission leaves earth for space station Mir. On board is a doctor who will check the health of the 2 cosmonauts who have been in space since last December.
TUESDAY August 30	So far this year, 66,895 forest fires have burned 3,400,000 acres throughout the United States. It's the worst year for fires since 1919!
WEDNESDAY August 31	The Afghan-Soviet spacecraft docks with the orbiting Mir. • 50 blocks of downtown Seattle, Washington, lose electricity during the worst blackout in the city's history.

VICE PRESIDENT GEORGE BUSH NOMINATED FOR PRESIDENT BY REPUBLICANS

FLOODING IN BANGLADESH LEAVES 25,000,000 HOMELESS

$1,000 WASHES UP ON RHODE ISLAND BEACH

2,000 BATS INVADE HOME IN NEW LONDON, NY

September

*T*he name September comes from the Latin *septem*, meaning "seven." This was the seventh month of the old Roman calendar.

BIRTHSTONE *Sapphire*

THURSDAY
September 1

16-year-old giant panda Chia-Chia leaves the London Zoo for the U.S., on his way to meet his new mate, Tohui, in Mexico City.

FRIDAY
September 2

The crew of space shuttle *Discovery* has just finished a 56-hour simulation (practice) to get ready for the launch of the new shuttle later this month.

SATURDAY
September 3

With his mouth, Paul Tavilla catches a grape that is dropped 788 feet from the top of a 60-story building in Boston, Massachusetts, breaking his old record in the *Guinness Book of World Records*.

SUNDAY
September 4

A lifeguard on Long Island, Vincent Rodomistor, swims through fog and heavy seas to save a man clinging to a disabled boat.

MONDAY
September 5

Labor Day • At the National Frisbee Disk Festival in Washington, D.C., 579 Frisbees are thrown at once!

TUESDAY
September 6

11-year-old Thomas Gregory from London, England, becomes the youngest person to swim across the English Channel. It takes him 11 hours, 45 minutes.

WEDNESDAY
September 7

In Milford, Connecticut, Catherine Pollard becomes the first female Boy Scout troop leader.

THURSDAY
September 8

Mumps is on the decline: only 3,166 cases reported in the U.S. in the first 30 weeks of 1988.

FRIDAY
September 9

An 80-pound propeller that fell off an airplane last week is found in the woods in Winhall, Vermont. • The U.S. wins the America's Cup yacht race.

FUN FACT '88

There are about 5,900,000 followers of Confucianism (the teachings of Confucius) in the world.

WHO ELSE WAS BORN IN SEPTEMBER?
CONFUCIUS (born K'UNG FU-TZU)
Chinese philosopher

The most important thinker in Chinese history, he spent his life teaching his philosophy of peace, order, kindness, wisdom, courage, and fidelity. His disciples collected his beliefs in a famous book of sayings, the *Analects*. BORN September 28, 551 B.C., in the state of Lu (now Shantung Province). No one knows exactly when he was born, but his birthday is always celebrated on this day.

SATURDAY
September 10

Steffi Graf wins the grand slam of tennis with her victory in the U.S. Open today. *Grand slam* means that this year she's also won 3 other major championships: the French Open, the Australian Open, and Wimbledon.

SUNDAY
September 11

Rosh Hashanah begins at sundown • Grandparents' Day • Mats Wilander wins the men's singles U.S. Open tennis championship, beating Ivan Lendl. Their match lasts a record 4 hours, 54 minutes.

MONDAY
September 12

Hurricane Gilbert hits Jamaica with 115-mile-per-hour winds: 500,000 people are left homeless. It's so strong that it is designated a Category 5 hurricane—only the 3d this century!

TUESDAY
September 13

Hurricane Gilbert hits the Cayman Islands in the Caribbean Sea at 130 miles per hour, leaving 60,000 people homeless.

WEDNESDAY
September 14

83,000 students in Michigan, Pennsylvania, Ohio, Illinois, and Massachusetts are still on summer vacation—their teachers are on strike.

THURSDAY
September 15

Weekly Reader celebrates its 60th anniversary with a book, published today: *Weekly Reader: 60 Years of News for Kids.*

FRIDAY
September 16

At a festival in the Netherlands, the world's largest working telephone is displayed. It's 8 feet, 1 inch high and 19 feet, 11 inches long, and the handset has to be lifted by a crane in order to make a call!

ANCIENT TOMB DISCOVERED IN PERU

In September, a 1,500-year-old tomb is found 420 miles northwest of Lima, Peru. It contains the remains of a warrior-priest of the Moche people, along with some of his wives and servants. The Moche Indians were a great civilization that lived in Peru before the Incas, from about A.D. 100 to 700. They were warlike but also were good farmers and craftspeople.

The skeleton in the tomb shows that the warrior-priest was in his 30s when he died. The bones of 2 women, 3 men, and 1 dog lie beside him. More than 100 pieces of fancy clothing and ceramics are also in the tomb. The Moche lord is covered in fine jewelry of gold, silver, and turquoise, and on his chest is a shield of pure gold that weighs 2 pounds.

SATURDAY
September 17
More than 12,000 dancers, 1,000 tae kwon do fighters, and 32 sky divers open the games of the XXIVth Summer Olympic Games in Seoul, South Korea.

SUNDAY
September 18
Snow falls in Yellowstone National Park, slowing the forest fires a little. The park has already lost 1,000,000 acres of trees. Fires throughout the West and in Alaska have destroyed a total of about 4,000,000 acres.

MONDAY
September 19
Israel launches an experimental satellite called *Ofek* (which means "Horizon"). It will collect information on solar energy and on the earth's magnetic field.

TUESDAY
September 20
Yom Kippur begins at sundown • Astronomers at Cornell University in New York have discovered ice volcanoes on 2 moons of Uranus.

WEDNESDAY
September 21
The International Banana Festival begins in Fulton, Kentucky—featuring 1 ton of banana pudding.

THURSDAY
September 22
Autumn equinox • Tonight Mars makes its closest approach to Earth—the nearest it's been in 17 years—about 36,000,000 miles away.

FRIDAY
September 23
In Great Britain, the largest leatherback turtle ever found washes ashore; it is 9 feet, 5½ inches long and weighs 2,016 pounds!

SATURDAY
September 24
An engineer named J. Turner Hunt has received a patent for a 5-bladed boomerang that travels in a straight line, then flips over and flies straight back.

SUMMER OLYMPICS SCORES

The XXIVth Summer Olympics are held in Seoul, South Korea, from September 17 to October 2. A record number of athletes take part—13,674, from 161 nations. The next games will be in Spain in 1992.

THE TOP 5 WINNERS

Soviet Union	132 medals:	55 gold, 31 silver, 46 bronze
East Germany	102 medals:	37 gold, 35 silver, 30 bronze
United States	94 medals:	36 gold, 31 silver, 27 bronze
West Germany	40 medals:	11 gold, 14 silver, 15 bronze
Bulgaria	35 medals:	10 gold, 12 silver, 13 bronze

SUNDAY
September 25
Full Moon

100,000,000 people watch a debate on TV between presidential candidates George Bush and Michael Dukakis.

MONDAY
September 26

French mountain climber Marc Batard sets a record by scaling Mount Everest, the world's highest mountain, in just 22 hours, 30 minutes.

TUESDAY
September 27

At the Summer Olympics in Korea, Greg Louganis wins the 3-meter springboard event and becomes the first diver in history to win gold medals in consecutive Olympics. (He won the same event in the 1984 Olympics.)

WEDNESDAY
September 28

Orel Hershiser of the Los Angeles Dodgers pitches 10 shutout innings against the San Diego Padres. This completes a total of 59 consecutive scoreless innings he has pitched, breaking the world record set in 1968.

THURSDAY
September 29

On the first shuttle mission since the explosion of *Challenger* in 1986, U.S. space shuttle *Discovery* lifts off from Cape Canaveral, Florida, carrying a 5-person crew.

FRIDAY
September 30

The late John Lennon, member of the Beatles rock and roll group, receives a star on the Hollywood Walk of Fame.

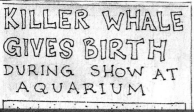

KILLER WHALE GIVES BIRTH DURING SHOW AT AQUARIUM

FIRST U.S. FEMALE ANGLICAN BISHOP ORDAINED

CHINA TO GET PIZZA HUT IN BEIJING

October

October was the eighth month of the old Roman calendar; the name is from the Latin *octo*, meaning "eight."

BIRTHSTONE *Opal*

SATURDAY
October 1

A horde of tiny toads invades part of New Port Richey, Florida. Some buildings' doors are blocked by hundreds of toads.

SUNDAY
October 2

Sarah Covington-Fulcher, who began her run around the United States on July 21, 1987, arrives in Los Angeles, California. She has run 11,134 miles around the perimeter of the U.S., the longest run ever by an individual.

MONDAY
October 3

A crowd of 400,000 watches as space shuttle *Discovery* lands at Edwards Air Force Base in California, after successfully deploying a communications satellite.

TUESDAY
October 4

Cherokee Indians meet in Cherokee, North Carolina, to mark the 150th anniversary of their eviction from the Southeast. In 1838, 18,000 of them were forced to move from their homelands and travel to Oklahoma. 4,000 died on the 7-month journey.

WEDNESDAY
October 5

LIVE FROM OMAHA: Candidates for vice president of the United States, Senator Lloyd Bentsen and Senator Dan Quayle, have a debate on TV.

THURSDAY
October 6

65 countries agree to ban the burning of chemicals at sea by the end of 1994.

FRIDAY
October 7

TO THE RESCUE: Eskimos discover 3 young California gray whales trapped beneath the ice off Point Barrow in northern Alaska. They cut air holes in the ice to help the whales breathe.

SATURDAY
October 8

The 70 workers at the Eiffel Tower in Paris, France, go on strike. They want a pay raise of about 31 cents an hour.

SUNDAY
October 9

Samuel Cottrell of Valley Center, California, has invented an alarm for swimming pools! It goes off if someone, such as a child or pet, falls into the water when no one is watching.

WHO ELSE WAS BORN IN OCTOBER?
NAT TURNER

American slave and preacher
He led the most important slave revolt in U.S.
history, the Southampton Insurrection, in 1831.
BORN October 2, 1800, in Southampton County,
Virginia

MONDAY
October 10

Columbus Day • Lanny Harbord from Nova Scotia, Canada, wins the World Pumpkin Confederation contest in Collins, New York, with a mammoth pumpkin weighing 627 pounds. A 653½-pound squash and a 187-pound watermelon also take top prizes.

TUESDAY
October 11

14 riverboats are paddling to Cincinnati for the Tall Stacks Celebration this weekend, part of the city's bicentennial festivities. • Eleanor Roosevelt was born on this day in 1884.

WEDNESDAY
October 12

200,000 people trying to get to work are stranded in New York City when a water main in midtown Manhattan breaks, flooding subway tunnels as far away as Queens with water up to 9 feet deep.

A WHALE OF A RESCUE

In October, 3 young California gray whales are discovered trapped in the Arctic ice off Point Barrow, Alaska. The cold weather came early, and the whales didn't migrate south in time! The Eskimos name them Pouto ("Ice Hole"), Siku ("Ice"), and Kanik ("Snowflake").

For 3 weeks, U.S. scientists, local Eskimos, the Alaska National Guard, and other groups join forces to try to free the whales. Even President Reagan calls to see how the whales are doing. Teams of people work around the clock poking, sawing, and hammering holes in the ice so the whales can breathe. A helicopter chops holes by repeatedly dropping a 5-ton concrete cylinder on the ice. On October 24, Soviet ice-breaking ships arrive; by October 28, they have cut a channel connecting the whales to the open sea. Unfortunately, the smallest, Kanik, is missing by this time, but the other 2 escape into the North Pacific.

Gray whales are an endangered species. They can reach 50 feet in length and can live for 70 years.

THURSDAY
October 13

A giant swarm of locusts—stretching for 400 miles—arrives in Saudi Arabia. • An underground nuclear weapons test at Yucca Flat, Nevada, causes buildings to sway 80 miles away in Las Vegas!

FRIDAY
October 14

Workers at the Eiffel Tower have ended their strike. They got a 6 percent raise in pay.

SATURDAY
October 15

World Poetry Day • Over 10,000 people attend the Apple Butter Stirrin' Festival in Coshocton, Ohio. The apple butter is cooked the old-fashioned way—in large kettles over open fires.

SUNDAY
October 16

The 3 California gray whales are still trapped in the ice near Point Barrow, Alaska. Eskimo hunters and the National Guard saw more holes in the ice so they can breathe.

MONDAY
October 17

Ikuo Hiyakuta of Japan wins the world Monopoly championship in London. During the championship, a new version of the game is unveiled: Russian monopoly (*Monopoliia*). The play money is in rubles.

TUESDAY
October 18

Using a telescope in the Canary Islands, astronomers have found gigantic whirlpools on the surface of the sun!

WEDNESDAY
October 19

Mayor Johnny Ford of Tuskegee, Alabama, is stuck for 3 hours in a pine tree, kept there by 2 snarling pit bulls.

THURSDAY
October 20

The Los Angeles Dodgers beat the Oakland Athletics in baseball's World Series, 4 games to 1.

FRIDAY
October 21

"Happy Birthday to You" is for sale by the Sengstack family of New Jersey, which owns the copyright to the song.

SATURDAY
October 22

In San Diego, California, the world's biggest Lego house is put together by a team of architects using 1,000,000 Lego bricks and special parts.

SUNDAY
October 23

More than 3,500 rowers in 850 boats compete in the largest rowing event in the U.S.—the Boston Head of the Charles Race, which takes place along a 3-mile section of the Charles River. The winner: the Penn Athletic Club, in 15 minutes, 15.31 seconds.

FUN FACT '88

The honeybee eats a substance it manufactures in the hive, a kind of "bread" made from pollen, 107 molds, 81 yeasts, and 39 kinds of bacteria.

MONDAY
October 24

BEE WEAR: U.S. bee researchers have started gluing tiny bar codes (like the ones on items in a supermarket) to the backs of bees! With the help of a computer, experts will be able to study the bees' habits more closely.

TUESDAY
October 25

Full Moon

2 letters, 2 small photographs, and 1 postcard sent by Anne Frank to pen pals in Danville, Iowa, in 1940 are sold at auction for $165,000 in New York City.

WEDNESDAY
October 26

In St. Paul Park, Minnesota, a baby is born whose full name is Eric Michael David Stephen Joshua Kevin Carl Quentin Jesse Alexander William Peters!

THURSDAY
October 27

8,000,000 copies of the video of *E.T.: The Extraterrestrial* are shipped to video stores all over the U.S.

FRIDAY
October 28

A Soviet icebreaker finishes cutting a path through the Arctic ice to free the California gray whales that have been trapped for 3 weeks in Alaska.

SATURDAY
October 29

59 years ago today, the stock market crashed and the Great Depression began.

SUNDAY
October 30

A nuclear reactor at the Three Mile Island plant in Pennsylvania automatically shuts itself down. There may be a problem in the turbine system.

MONDAY
October 31

Halloween. This year's top-selling costumes are Alf, Roger Rabbit, Pee Wee Herman, Freddy Kruger, California Raisin, E.T., Beetlejuice, and Darth Vader. Kids' favorite treat: chocolate candy bars.

MAN SMUGGLES 700 BOA CONSTRICTORS OUT OF SOUTH AMERICA	SKATEBOARDING BANNED IN LOCKPORT, NY	$60,800,000 LOTTO JACKPOT AWARDED IN CALIFORNIA	HURRICANE JOAN HITS NICARAGUA

November

November was the ninth month of the old Roman calendar. The name comes from the Latin *novem*, meaning "nine."

BIRTHSTONE *Topaz*

TUESDAY
November 1

A new study released today from the University of Southern California says that people think better standing up.

WEDNESDAY
November 2

A computer virus is discovered in a U.S. Defense Department system in California. It closes down 6,000 computers and affects many others.

THURSDAY
November 3

Bug expert Edgar Shaw has invented a gigantic vacuum cleaner for sucking insects off strawberries in a strawberry patch. It's called the Bugvac.

FRIDAY
November 4

Video stores everywhere are sold out of *E.T.: The Extraterrestrial*; all 8,000,000 copies shipped last week were bought.

SATURDAY
November 5

Charles Walker breaks a world record by playing 201 games of checkers simultaneously in New Orleans, Louisiana. • At a TV studio in Australia, Luis Salamanca sets a new yo-yo speed record— 7,574 loops in an hour.

SUNDAY
November 6

The women's race in the New York City Marathon is won by Grete Waitz of Norway—for the ninth time! She finishes in 2 hours, 28 minutes, 7 seconds. The men's winner is Steve Jones of Wales, with a time of 2 hours, 8 minutes, 20 seconds.

SICK COMPUTERS

A computer "virus" is a set of instructions hidden in a computer system. The virus usually wipes out stored information, and it is made so that it is secretly transmitted from computer to computer. In November 1988, a very contagious virus spreads through many computers in the U.S. A 23-year-old Cornell University student, Robert Morris, Jr., designed it. Computers at top universities and military labs throughout the nation are shut down until computer scientists can find a cure.

WHO ELSE WAS BORN IN NOVEMBER?
SHIRLEY CHISHOLM

U.S. politician and educator
In 1968, she became the first black woman to be elected to the House of Representatives. She also ran for president of the United States in 1972, winning 10 percent of the votes at the Democratic convention.
BORN November 30, 1924, in Brooklyn, New York

MONDAY
November 7

To get people ready to celebrate Mickey Mouse's 60th birthday on November 18, a 32-page advertisement appears in *Time* magazine. The ad cost Walt Disney $3,851,684!

TUESDAY
November 8

Vice President George Bush is elected president of the United States. He takes office in January 1989.

WEDNESDAY
November 9

Frank Viola of the Minnesota Twins receives the Cy Young Award for being the American League's outstanding pitcher of 1988.

THURSDAY
November 10

Orel Hershiser of the Los Angeles Dodgers wins the National League Cy Young Award for pitching.

FRIDAY
November 11

Radio commands are sent from Earth to the *Voyager 2* space probe to change its course and head it toward Neptune. It's 2.6 billion miles away; radio signals take 4 hours to reach it!

SATURDAY
November 12

The town with the longest name in Great Britain, Llanfairpwllgwyngyllgogerychwyrndrobwllllantysi-liogogogoch, has shortened it to Llanfair Pwllgwyngyll to make life a bit easier.

SUNDAY
November 13

Scientists discover the world's oldest known insect. It lived more than 390,000,000 years ago and was preserved in a piece of mudstone in Quebec, Canada.

MONDAY
November 14

A painting by Pablo Picasso is auctioned in New York City for $24,800,000. • Happy 40th birthday to Prince Charles of Great Britain.

HAPPY BIRTHDAY, MICKEY!

To celebrate the 60th birthday of America's favorite mouse, Mickey's Birthdayland in the Magic Kingdom opens at Disney World in Florida. In 240 acres of farmland in Iowa, a gigantic profile of Mickey's head is cut into the corn so that it's visible from an airplane. A 125-foot-high Mickey Mouse hot-air balloon tours the U.S. It has a 33-foot-long nose and 16-foot-high eyes, and it's called "Ear Force One." In October, Mickey makes his very first appearance in Moscow, for the first Soviet festival of Walt Disney animated classics.

On Mickey's actual birthday on November 18, some 4,000 children join Mickey and Minnie and parade down Main Street, USA, at Disney World in Florida. Minnie is 60 this year too!

TUESDAY
November 15

The first Soviet space shuttle, *Buran* ("Snowstorm"), takes off and orbits Earth twice in 3 hours, 25 minutes. It is unmanned. • 49 tornadoes sweep through 5 states in the U.S.

WEDNESDAY
November 16

Patrick Guillanton catches a record-breaking mako shark—1,115 pounds—in the Black River in Mauritius.

THURSDAY
November 17

The oldest fossil reptile in the world—Lizzie the Lizard—goes on display in London, England. She is 340,000,000 years old and was found in Scotland.

FRIDAY
November 18

Happy birthday, Mickey Mouse. He made his debut in the first talkie cartoon, *Steamboat Willie*, 60 years ago today.

SATURDAY
November 19

Basketball star Larry Bird of the Boston Celtics has surgery to remove bone spurs from his heels.

SUNDAY
November 20

The World Cup of Pastry competition in Bethesda, Maryland, is won by Anne Johnson of Carlstadt, New Jersey. Her pastries have ribbons, leaves, and branches—all made out of candy!

MONDAY
November 21

2 loggerhead turtles at the National Aquarium in Baltimore, Maryland, have been named George and Barbara, after the soon-to-be President and First Lady.

FUN FACT '88

A total of 22,500,000 people visit Disney World this year.

TUESDAY
November 22

The new U.S. B2 Stealth bomber is unveiled in California. It is made of special radar-absorbent material so that it can slip through enemy defenses. It was kept top secret for 7 years.

WEDNESDAY
November 23

Full Moon

A pair of dolphins, Nimo and Limo, are flown from a hotel swimming pool in Cairo, Egypt, to an aquarium in Antibes, France. The hotel manager says they were abandoned; the dolphins' owner says they were kidnapped.

THURSDAY
November 24

Thanksgiving Day • 15-year-old Karen Brecher of Tenafly, New Jersey, has received a patent for a Velcro brace designed to keep shoelaces tied.

FRIDAY
November 25

LOVE MATCH: The captain of the U.S. chess team marries one of the U.S.S.R.'s top players during the Chess Olympiad in Greece. They met and fell in love at a chess match in Cuba in 1985.

SATURDAY
November 26

The Soviet Union launches a new 3-person mission to *Mir*, the orbiting space station.

SUNDAY
November 27

A painting by Edouard Manet worth $1,000,000 is stolen from a museum in Huntington, New York.

MONDAY
November 28

THE GRINCH WHO GOT STUCK: Fire fighters find a burglar wedged inside a chimney in Los Angeles, California. He is calling for help.

TUESDAY
November 29

Gordon Kennel of Montana has invented a folding sled. It folds up to the size of a briefcase.

WEDNESDAY
November 30

The Manet painting stolen Sunday is found in a laundry room in a New York City apartment building.

POWERFUL EARTHQUAKE ROCKS YUNNAN PROVENCE IN CHINA

REMAINS OF ABORIGINAL TOOLS FOUND IN AUSTRALIA

U.S. TITAN 34D ROCKET BLASTS OFF ON SECRET MISSION

KILLER BEES FOUND ON SHIP DOCKED IN TAMPA, FLORIDA

December

*D*ecember used to be the tenth month of the year (the Latin *decem* means "ten"). The old Roman calendar began with March.

BIRTHSTONE *Turquoise*

THURSDAY
December 1

Archaeologists in South Africa have found evidence of humans' early use of fire—1,500,000-year-old charred fossilized animal bones from ancient campfires.

FRIDAY
December 2

9:30 A.M.: U.S. space shuttle *Atlantis* takes off from Cape Canaveral, Florida, with a 5-person crew.
• Benazir Bhutto is inaugurated as president of Pakistan. She is the first woman in modern history to govern a Muslim nation.

SATURDAY
December 3

First night of Hanukkah • Barry Sanders, a tailback for Oklahoma State, receives the Heisman Trophy for outstanding college football player.

SUNDAY
December 4

10,000,000 Nintendo systems have been sold to date in the U.S.

MONDAY
December 5

The town of Milford, Connecticut, bans skateboarding in the business district.

TUESDAY
December 6

Space shuttle *Atlantis* returns to earth at Edwards Air Force Base in California. During their 5-day mission, the crew deployed a new spy satellite.

WEDNESDAY
December 7

President Reagan, President-elect Bush, and Soviet leader Gorbachev have lunch together on Governors Island in New York. • Major earthquake in Armenia—6.9 on the Richter scale.

THURSDAY
December 8

The Ho Ho Ho hot line opens today. Kids wanting to talk to Santa or Mrs. Claus can call.

FUN FACT '88

50,500,000 Cabbage Patch dolls have been sold since 1978.

WHO ELSE WAS BORN IN DECEMBER?
SIR ISAAC NEWTON

English scientist, mathematician
He had one of the greatest scientific minds in history.
Known for his laws of motion and his law of gravity,
Newton was also the first to show that white light
was actually a combination of all colors.
BORN   December 25, 1642, in Woolsthorpe, England

FRIDAY
December 9

Astronomers have discovered that the planet Pluto has an atmosphere, probably of methane gas. • 7 large pythons—big enough to eat a small child—have been found in Oldsmar, Florida.

SATURDAY
December 10

The largest doughnut in the world is made in Crystal River, Florida. It is lemon-filled, weighs 2,099 pounds, and is 22 feet in diameter.

SUNDAY
December 11

The European Space Agency's *Ariane 4* rocket takes off from French Guiana with the new *Astra* TV satellite on board.

MONDAY
December 12

Jean-Loup Chretien becomes the first French person to walk in space, outside the orbiting space station *Mir*.

TUESDAY
December 13

3 paintings by Dutch artist Vincent van Gogh are stolen from a museum in the Netherlands. • An Indian merchant ship is accidentally hit by a practice missile launched by the U.S. Navy.

WEDNESDAY
December 14

At Cap de Garde in Algeria, Jean Yves Chatard catches a 35-pound, 2-ounce little tunny, a record for a fish of this kind.

THURSDAY
December 15

Bill of Rights Day • In Spain, more than 7,000,000 workers are on strike, protesting government policies on wages and prices.

TOY BOX '88
Hottest Christmas toys

Nintendo games
Teenage Mutant Ninja Turtles
Dinosaurs
Stuffed rabbits (especially Roger Rabbit)
Motorized Mighty Tonka Tow Truck
Play-Doh Fingles

Gigantik Snakes and Ladders
Hot Wheels Color Racers
 Auto Paint Factory
Playskool Express train set
Etch A Sketch Animator 2000
Hula hoops

Top Dolls

Dr. Barbie	Toni	Cowgirl
Asian Just Born	April	Snow White and the 7 Dwarfs
Little Arthur	Martina	Tiffany
L'il Miss Makeup	Melinda	Baby Grows
Gigi	Cynthia	

FRIDAY
December 16

Youti Kuo of Renfield, New York, has invented a toothbrush for the handicapped—it dispenses its own toothpaste and requires the use of only one hand.

SATURDAY
December 17

A company in Tokyo, Japan, has received a patent for an indoor ski slope. It would fit inside a large building and would wind around a central tower.

SUNDAY
December 18

The world's largest paper airplane—with a wingspan of 10 feet—is made and flown for 70 feet in Zurich, Switzerland.

MONDAY
December 19

Soviet cosmonauts Vladimir Titov and Musa Manarov leave the space station *Mir*, where they've been since December 20, 1987. They have spent 365 days, 22 hours, and 39 minutes in orbit, breaking the space endurance record set by Yuri Romanenko last year.

TUESDAY
December 20

In an experiment to study ancient civilizations, archaeologist Gil Stein plunges part of a 4,500-year-old bowl into the core of a nuclear reactor in Gaithersburg, Maryland.

WEDNESDAY
December 21

Winter solstice • The *Soyuz TM-6* spacecraft carrying a Soviet-French crew touches down in Central Asia. • Today is the 75th birthday of the crossword puzzle, created by Arthur Wynne for the *New York World* in 1913. It was called a wordcross.

THURSDAY
December 22

A bottlenose dolphin nicknamed Rascal seems to be stranded in the cold waters off Virginia Beach, Virginia. It should have gone south with the other dolphins. Marine experts are planning to rescue the lost dolphin.

FRIDAY
December 23
Full Moon

A candlelight tour is held at the White House from 6:00 to 8:00 in the evening, so that visitors can see the presidential Christmas decorations.

And right this way is Mr. Lincoln's bedroom!

CHRISTMAS TREE CORNER

did you know that
36 percent of people in the U.S. buy live trees.
36 percent buy artificial trees.
28 percent buy no tree.
The most popular Christmas tree is the Scotch pine!

SATURDAY
December 24

Christmas Eve • For $500 per home, an ice company in southern California is putting snow on houses and lawns for people who've never had a white Christmas!

SUNDAY
December 25

Christmas • 2 men who were trapped under 6 feet of snow—caused by an avalanche—are rescued in Durango, Colorado. People passing by heard them yell and saw a glove on the snow.

MONDAY
December 26

An American robin, blown across the Atlantic by westerly winds, is spotted in Grampian, England. It's almost twice as big as a European robin.

TUESDAY
December 27

More than $23,000,000 of plastic action figures of Teenage Mutant Ninja Turtles have been sold since June!

WEDNESDAY
December 28

In Chile, the volcano Lonquinay, which erupted 2 days ago for the first time in 100 years, sends gas, stones, and ash shooting into the air.

THURSDAY
December 29

On this day in 1845, Texas became a state; in 1848, gaslights were installed in the White House; and in 1851, the first YMCA in the U.S. opened in Boston, Massachusetts.

FRIDAY
December 30

The government of Canada officially agrees to a U.S./Canadian free-trade pact. The agreement will make it easier for the 2 countries to do business together.

SATURDAY
December 31

New Year's Eve • Donald Spector has received a patent for his new art form: sculptures made from candied popcorn.
• The Big Apple falls in Times Square in New York City while thousands cheer in the new year.

ARMED ROBBERS IN
POLICE UNIFORMS
STEAL $4,000,000
IN NEW JERSEY

PAN AM JET
CRASHES IN
SCOTLAND,
KILLING 258.

YOUR YEAR AT A GLANCE

A lot happened the year you were born. How many events shown on the cover can you identify? Turn the page upside down for the answers.

1. Rik Dunkan of Australia hang glides down Mount Fuji (August 10) **2.** The XV Winter Olympics are held at the city of Calgary in Alberta, Canada (see February) **3.** Fire fighters rescue boaters about to be swept over Niagara Falls (July 28) **4.** A team from Taiwan wins the Little League World Series in Williamsport, Pennsylvania (August 27) **5.** American pizza is sold in Russia for the first time (April 12) **6.** Butterfly World, the home of over 2,000 butterflies, opens in Coconut Creek, Florida (March 23) **7.** Dinosaurs are hot in 1988 (see July: What's Hot in 1988) **8.** Two loggerhead turtles at the National Aquarium have been named after President Bush and the First Lady (November 21) **9.** Experts in Egypt repair the Sphinx (March 1) **10.** A horde of tiny toads invades part of New Port Richey, Florida (October 1) **11.** Hurricane Gilbert hits Jamaica with 115 mph winds (September 12) **12.** The XXIV Summer Olympics are held in Seoul, South Korea (see September) **13.** Greg Louganis is the first diver to win consecutive gold medals in the Olympics (September 27) **14.** Stephen Venables of Great Britain is the first to climb the east face of Mount Everest without oxygen (May 12) **15.** Earthquakes shake Tokyo, Japan, and central Utah (August 12 & 14) **16.** Visitors to Universal Studio Tours in Hollywood can act in the new Star Trek Adventure set (June 1)